being a woman:

Celebrating the Nuances of Femininity in a
Changing World

Raw n Rosy

ISBN: 978-1-961902-02-2

Published By LitBooks

Printed in the United States of America

Cover design by Victor Oj

Editor and Illustrator: Elsie Bloomfield

Introduction...

this book of poetry seeks to shed light on the unique experiences and challenges faced by women. through sixty-five pages of evocative and emotionally resonant verse, this book delves deep into the struggles that women must often endure in a world that is too often indifferent to their pain.

from discrimination and inequality to the deeply personal struggles of love and loss, these poems explore the many facets of a woman's experience with a raw and unflinching honesty. but amidst the darkness and the pain, there is also hope and healing to be found.

through the power of poetic language and a deep understanding of the human soul, this book seeks to inspire and uplift women everywhere, reminding them of their inherent worth and strength, and offering a roadmap for finding the path towards healing and empowerment.

i invite you to journey with me through the pages of this book, to hear the voices of women who have been silenced for too long, and to feel the power of the human spirit as it rises up to meet the challenges of the world. this book is a tribute to the resilience and strength of women everywhere, and i hope that it will inspire you to find your own voice and your own path towards healing and wholeness.

Table of Contents

epigram...

in the garden of womanhood, there grows a tender rose,

petals soft and fragile, amidst life's highs and lows.

her roots run deep, her stem stands tall,

a testimony to strength, in the face of it all.

the pain

the thorns of her life, they pierce and they sting,

a mother's lament, the heartache they bring.

the weight of the world, on her shoulders it lies,

the tears in her eyes, the unspoken goodbyes.

the shards of glass, of a broken dream,

a lover's betrayal, an unheard scream.

her body a canvas, of scars unseen,

the pain she endures, to keep her soul clean.

- her agony

her life, a tightrope, expectations abound,

conforming to roles, in society's playground.

the pressure to please, to be perfect and poised,

a cage of ideals, where her spirit is hoisted.

the daughter, the sister, the mother, the wife,

each label a duty, that dictates her life.

the dreams she once harbored, pushed aside and ignored,

for the sake of her loved ones, her heart left unmoored.

- burden of expectations

silent surrender, her day-to-day plight,

her wishes and desires, hidden from sight.

the sacrifices she makes, go unnoticed and unsung,

the price of her love, a story untold.

she gives up herself, a wellspring of care,

her energy drained, in the service of others.

her shoulders are strong, her spirit unbent,

as she carries the weight, of the world in her hands.

- unseen sacrifices

in a world that defines, by the color and shape,

her worth and her value, like shadows they escape.

the struggle for identity, a battle within,

against prejudice and bias, a war she must win.

her spirit, a phoenix, rises above the fray,

the pain of existence, she refuses to obey.

embracing her power, her uniqueness and grace,

she defies the conventions, she's more than a face.

-    struggle for identity

the violence she endures, both body and soul,

the scars she carries, a history untold.

for every woman who suffers, in silence she weeps,

her sisters in anguish, a vigil she keeps.

in the face of injustice, she stands resolute,

with courage and wisdom, her voice she'll not mute.

her pain is her armor, her anguish her shield,

as she fights for the future, and the world she will wield.

- scars of injustice

her heart, an ocean, with tides deep and vast,

the waves of emotion, in perpetual contrast.

the joy and the sorrow, the laughter and tears,

a complex symphony, as her journey appears.

she navigates storms, through life's tempestuous seas,

her vessel of courage, endures every breeze.

though battered and bruised, she soldiers on,

a beacon of resilience, from dusk until dawn.

- emotional tides

in the chambers of secrets, her voice locked away,

her whispers of anguish, left unspoken each day.

the pain she conceals, like a shadow it looms,

in the quiet of night, her heartache resumes.

her silent screams echo, in the depths of her soul,

a cavern of sorrow, an unending toll.

yet amidst the darkness, a glimmer of hope,

the key to her freedom, her strength to cope.

- weight of silence

bound by convention, by judgment and shame,

the chains of society, her spirit they tame.

the whispers and stares, the gossip and scorn,

a labyrinth of expectations, her heart left forlorn.

she wears the masks, her emotions concealed,

the smiles and the laughter, her armor to wield.

the pain she endures, a constant reminder,

of the battles she faces, as a brave survivor.

- chains of society

her path, a mosaic, of thorns and of stones,

the pain and the struggles, the heartaches and moans.

yet through every trial, she finds her way,

a warrior of spirit, with each passing day.

the chapters of sorrow, a testament to her strength,

her story a beacon, her courage at length.

the pain that she bears, a fire within,

a forge of resilience, her armor to win

- journey through adversity

her life, a tightrope, a delicate dance,

a quest for balance, amidst chaos and chance.

the demands of her roles, the expectations they bring,

a juggling act, as her heart takes wing.

the longing for peace, in a world full of strife,

a harmony sought, throughout her life.

the pain of imbalance, a weight on her chest,

yet, she finds her footing, in each daunting test.

- battle for balance

once vibrant and vivid, her dreams start to fade,

the aspirations of youth, now distant and frayed.

her heart aches with longing, for the passions once known,

the fire that burned, now embers wind-blown.

but even in loss, a spark still remains,

a glimmer of hope, that the flame will regain.

the pain of her dreams, a bittersweet refrain,

a reminder of courage, her spirit unchained.

- loss of dreams

her contributions, her worth, often left unrecognized,

an invisibility cloak, her efforts disguised.

her tears and her sweat, unseen by the world,

as she nurtures and loves, her wings unfurled.

the pain of neglect, a thorn in her side,

a silent ache, she tries to hide.

yet, she perseveres, her strength unwavering,

in the face of invisibility, her spirit unshaken.

-   invisibility cloak

the conflict within, a constant struggle,

a tug of war, between pain and resilience.

her heart caught in the middle, pulled to and fro,

as she searches for solace, for a place to call home.

in every challenge, she finds strength anew,

her pain transformed, as wisdom accrues.

a testament to fortitude, a beacon of light,

the woman who endures, her spirit takes flight.

- tug of war

the struggles

through the stormy weather, she fights and she strives,

each challenge a lesson, as she dances through life.

her hands may be calloused, her spirit unbowed,

in the fire of adversity, she's tempered and proud.

the chains that they place, to bind and control,

can't shackle the freedom, that burns in her soul.

her voice may be silenced, but her spirit sings true,

the chorus of women, their strength shining through.

- her struggles

her journey a mountain, with peaks steep and high,

each step she takes, toward the limitless sky.

the struggle for progress, an arduous climb,

yet, undeterred, she perseveres with each stride.

the rocks and the boulders, the obstacles she faces,

with courage and grace, she conquers each challenge.

through the storm and the fog, her vision remains clear,

her spirit, a compass, guiding her near.

- the uphill climb

in a world that divides, by gender and creed,

her battle for fairness, a just cause indeed.

her voice in the chorus, demanding change,

a tireless advocate, for a world rearranged.

the struggle for rights, for respect and worth,

a woman empowered, an unyielding force.

her passion unwavering, her convictions strong,

the pursuit of equality, her life's noble song.

- fight for equality

her dreams and ambitions, a fire burning bright,

the struggle for opportunity, her unyielding fight.

the doors that are closed, the paths that are barred,

yet, she finds the courage, to challenge and discard.

the barriers she faces, both subtle and stark,

cannot dampen her spirit, nor extinguish her spark.

her quest undeterred, she seeks a better way,

a world of possibilities, where her dreams can play.

- quest for opportunity

her roles interwoven, a complex tapestry,

the struggle for balance, a constant decree.

the mother, the partner, the worker, the friend,

each aspect of life, a delicate blend.

she strives for a harmony, amidst chaos and change,

her strength and resilience, her love rearranged.

the dance of her life, a symphony of grace,

the struggles she faces, with courage embraced.

- balance of life

in the whirlwind of life, she tends to others,

her children, her partner, her sisters and brothers.

the struggle for self-care, often left unattended,

her own needs and desires, neglected and
suspended.

she learns to find moments, to nourish her soul,

to seek out the solace, to make herself whole.

the balance of caring, for self and for others,

a delicate act, her spirit uncovers.

- battle of self-care

the eyes that scrutinize, the whispers that sting,

the struggle against judgment, an unending ring.

her choices, her actions, constantly appraised,

in the harsh light of opinion, her spirit left dazed.

yet, she stands tall and defiant, her resolve never swayed,

the judgments of others, left powerless and frayed.

her strength is her armor, her conviction her shield,

in the face of adversity, she refuses to yield.

- weight of judgment

her heart longs for kinship, for bonds that run deep,

the struggle for connection, a hill often steep.

the world can be cruel, and friendships can wane,

yet, she seeks out the warmth, the love to regain.

through the trials of life, she reaches out her hand,

in search of the ones, who'll truly understand.

the struggles she faces, the heartaches she bears,

are softened by love, and the bonds that she shares.

-    pursuit of connection

her mind, a battleground, where doubt wages war,

the struggle against fear, a burden she bore.

the whispers of uncertainty, the questions that taunt,

the battle for confidence, a persistent haunt.

but through every skirmish, her spirit holds fast,

the strength of her will, a beacon that lasts.

her struggles against doubt, a testament to her might,

a warrior of resilience, who'll never lose sight.

- war against doubt

in a world that dictates, who she ought to be,

the struggle for identity, a journey to see.

the labels and expectations, that cloud her sight,

a quest for self-discovery, a courageous fight.

she peels back the layers, the masks that she's worn,

to find the true essence, of the soul that's been torn.

in the struggle for identity, she rediscovers her worth,

the power within, a celestial rebirth.

- search for identity

to open her heart, to bare her soul,

the struggle for vulnerability, a journey untold.

the walls she has built, the armor she wears,

a fortress of strength, concealing her cares.

yet, she learns to embrace, the power within,

the courage to show, her true self to begin.

in the struggle for vulnerability, she finds her voice,

the freedom to express, her spirit's true choice.

-     challenge of vulnerability

the currents of life, ever shifting and swift,

the struggle to navigate change, a courageous lift.

the tides that transform, the seasons that pass,

a woman adapting, her spirit steadfast.

through the storms and the calm, she adjusts her sail,

her resilience a compass, guiding her trail.

the struggles she faces, the challenges she meets,

in the dance of change, her spirit completes.

- navigation of change

her life a mosaic, of triumphs and strife,

the struggle for resilience, the core of her life.

the hardships she faces, the battles she's fought,

a testament to strength, her spirit unbought.

through the fire of adversity, she's forged and refined,

a warrior of courage, her heart unconstrained.

the struggles she endures, a beacon of light,

a woman empowered; her spirit takes flight.

- endurance of resilience

in the face of doubt, where others may falter,

the struggle for self-belief, a challenge she'll alter.

the whispers of insecurity, the voices that jeer,

her conviction remains steadfast, her purpose clear.

she silences the naysayers, with courage untold,

her belief in herself, a power uncontrolled.

in the struggle for self-belief, she forges her path,

a force to be reckoned, her spirit's own craft.

-    fight for self-belief

in the chaos of life, the search for contentment,

the struggle for happiness, a constant commitment.

the moments of sorrow, the trials she endures,

yet, she seeks out the joy, her heart reassures.

she finds solace in laughter, in love, and in peace,

her quest for happiness, an unending release.

the struggles she faces, the battles she braves,

a testament to resilience, her spirit engraves.

-   pursuit of happiness

in the shadow of fear, she faces her demons,

the struggle against terror, her courage deepens.

the nightmares that haunt, the doubts that arise,

in the face of adversity, her spirit defies.

she conquers her fears, with bravery untold,

her strength and her courage, a story unfold.

in the struggle against fear, her resolve shines bright,

a beacon of hope, her spirit's own light.

- conquest of fear

in the mirror of life, her reflection she sees,

the struggle for acceptance, a quest to appease.

the flaws and the beauty, the scars and the grace,

she learns to embrace, with a loving embrace.

she finds in herself, the love she deserves,

the acceptance she seeks, her spirit observes.

the struggles she faces, in the journey to find,

the love for herself, a treasure divine.

- journey of acceptance

the tapestry of connections, intricate and vast,

the struggle to nurture relationships, a lifetime amassed.

the threads that entwine, the bonds that endure,

her love and her care, a balm to ensure.

through the complexities of life, she weaves her web,

the struggles in relationships, her spirit to ebb.

the love that she gives, the bridges she mends,

her heart ever open, her spirit transcends.

- web of relationships

the lines that she draws, the borders she sets,

the struggle for boundaries, her spirit begets.

to protect her own space, her heart, and her mind,

a fortress of self, her strength underlined.

in the face of intrusion, she stands firm and tall,

her boundaries unyielding, a safeguarding wall.

the struggles she endures, in the battle to claim,

her own sacred ground, her spirit aflame.

- battle for boundaries

the trials she encounters, the challenges she meets,

in the struggle for growth, her spirit completes.

the pain and the sorrow, the setbacks she braves,

a catalyst for change, her resilience paves.

she rises above, the heartaches and strife,

transformed and renewed, in the crucible of life.

through the struggles she faces, her spirit evolves,

a testament to growth, her journey resolves.

- growth through adversity

heartbreak

a love once so tender, now turned to stone,

the echo of laughter, that once was her own.

her heart lies in pieces, a jigsaw unsolved,

a story of loss, of a love unresolved.

she mourns for the children, she could not embrace,

the life that was stolen, by time's cruel pace.

yet within her heartbreak, a seed starts to grow,

a promise of healing, a new hope to sow.

- her heart breaks

in the silent hours, when the world is asleep,

her heart, it aches, and her soul begins to weep.

the dreams that were shattered, the hopes torn apart,

a symphony of sorrow, playing within her heart.

she mourns for the loss, the paths left untraveled,

the heartbreak she bears, a burden unraveled.

yet, through the darkness, a light starts to glow,

a beacon of resilience, her spirit will show.

- shattered dreams

the love that once flowed, like a river so deep,

now ebbs and retreats, her heart left to weep.

the bond that once tethered, two souls intertwined,

now severed and broken, her spirit confined.

in the wake of heartbreak, she searches for meaning,

the love that was lost, her soul left grieving.

but through the sorrow, her strength starts to rise,

a phoenix emerging, her spirit defies.

- ebbing love

the trust that was shattered, the loyalty scorned,

the heartbreak of betrayal, a wound deeply mourned.

her faith in others, once steadfast and sure,

now fractured and splintered, her spirit unsure.

in the shadow of deceit, she finds her resolve,

to heal from the pain, her heart to absolve.

the heartbreak of betrayal, a fire within,

to forge her resilience, her spirit will win.

- betrayal's sting

the friends that depart, the bonds that dissolve,

the heartbreak of loss, a mystery to solve.

the laughter and memories, now echoes of the past,

a tapestry of love, her spirit amassed.

she cherishes the moments, the love that once thrived,

the connections now faded; her heart has survived.

in the heartbreak of loss, she finds solace and peace,

her spirit renewed, her strength to release.

- lost connections

the innocence stolen, the purity marred,

the heartbreak of loss, her spirit scarred.

the world once so vibrant, now dulled by life's sting,

a melancholy chorus, her heart starts to sing.

yet, within the darkness, a light starts to gleam,

a spark of resilience, her spirit to redeem.

in the heartbreak of loss, she finds strength anew,

her spirit unbroken, her heart's courage to pursue.

- loss of innocence

the distance that grows, between hearts once so near,

the heartbreak of separation, a pain to endear.

the longing for closeness, the ache to belong,

a symphony of sorrow, her spirit's forlorn song.

in the midst of heartache, she finds solace in memories,

the love that still lingers, her spirit to appease.

the heartbreak of separation, a journey to mend,

her spirit resilient, her heart on the mend.

- pain of separation

a silent chamber, her heartache confined,

the heartbreak of loneliness, her spirit maligned.

the yearning for solace, a voice to be heard,

a tender embrace, her soul's fervent word.

in the quietude of sorrow, she uncovers her might,

a blossoming resilience, her spirit ignites.

the heartbreak of loneliness, a catalyst for change,

her spirit unshackled, her life rearranged.

- echoes of loneliness

the image distorted, a mirror of pain,

the heartbreak of self-doubt, her spirit restrained.

the worth she once cherished, now fractured and marred,

a battle within, her soul deeply scarred.

yet, through the storm of despair, she uncovers her light,

a radiant beacon, her spirit takes flight.

the heartbreak of self-doubt, a hurdle surpassed,

her spirit triumphant, her confidence amassed.

- fractured reflection

the touch that once warmed, now cold and withdrawn,

the heartbreak of distance, her spirit forlorn.

the comfort once given, a memory fading,

a tenderness lost; her soul left craving.

in the void of despair, she summons her power,

a blossoming resilience, her spirit's finest hour.

the heartbreak of distance, a challenge to surmount,

her spirit indomitable, her courage paramount.

-     fading embrace

the words left unspoken, the feelings suppressed,

the heartbreak of silence, her spirit oppressed.

the longing to share, the ache to confide,

a secret burden, her soul to divide.

amidst the hush of sorrow, she finds her voice anew,

a symphony of strength, her spirit to imbue.

the heartbreak of silence, a barrier transcended,

her spirit unchained, her heartstrings mended.

- unspoken words

the burdens she bears, like mountains of stone,

the heartbreak of responsibility, her spirit bemoans.

the weight of the world, upon her shoulders to rest,

a pressure unyielding, her heart to contest.

amidst the toil of sorrow, she unearths her might,

a pillar of resilience, her spirit's true sight.

the heartbreak of responsibility, a test to withstand,

her spirit undaunted, her strength to command.

- weight of the world

healing

in the garden of grief, where her heart lay in tatters,

a phoenix emerges, as the darkness scatters.

her wounds may be deep, but her spirit renews,

in the warmth of the sun, her strength she renews.

a tapestry woven, of love and of loss,

each tear-stained memory, a lesson embossed.

the rose in the garden, now wiser and free,

blooms in the sunlight, a testament to thee.

so sing of the women, who rise and who fall,

their pain, their struggles, their heartbreak and all,

and remember the healing, the power within,

the strength of a woman, who refuses to give in.

-     hope sips in

through the veil of darkness, a glimmer emerges,

the healing of hope, her spirit encourages.

the shadows retreat, the sun starts to rise,

a radiant horizon, her heart's sweet surprise.

in the warmth of renewal, she finds solace and peace,

the healing of hope, her soul's sweet release.

a journey through heartache, a path to embrace,

her spirit uplifted, her heart's newfound grace.

- dawning light

a torrent of mercy, her heart to immerse,

the healing of forgiveness, her spirit's gentle verse.

the pain that once lingered, now washed away clean,

a newfound serenity, her soul's calming scene.

in the flow of absolution, she discovers her strength,

the healing of forgiveness, her heart's breadth and length.

a passage through sorrow, a transformation profound,

her spirit unburdened, her love unbound.

- river of forgiveness

in the soil of heartache, a seed starts to sprout,

the healing of growth, her spirit devout.

the pain that once festered, now fertile and lush,

a blossoming of wisdom, her heart's gentle hush.

through the verdant landscape, she finds her own way,

the healing of growth, her spirit's sunray.

a journey of self-discovery, a path to unveil,

her spirit enriched, her heart's tender tale.

- garden of growth

a melody of self-care, her heart to serenade,

the healing of self-love, her spirit's crusade.

the notes that once ached, now harmonious and sweet,

a resounding affirmation, her soul's rhythmic beat.

in the music of acceptance, she finds her own voice,

the healing of self-love, her spirit's true choice.

a voyage through heartbreak, a passage to embrace,

her spirit empowered, her heart's loving grace.

- symphony of self-love

the circle of life, the journey unending,

the tale of women, their strength unbending.

through trials and heartache, their spirits rise,

a chorus of resilience, their heart's sweet prize.

the healing that follows, a balm to mend,

the wounds of the past, their hearts to tend.

a testament to courage, their spirits soar,

an unbroken circle, forevermore.

- unbroken circle

a tapestry woven, with threads of gold,

the story of women, their strength untold.

through ages and eras, their courage shines bright,

a beacon of hope, their spirits alight.

in the healing embrace, of love and of care,

their wounds are tended, their hearts laid bare.

the tapestry of time, a testament to grace,

their spirits united, in life's sweet embrace.

- tapestry of time

the metamorphosis of women, a journey of change,

through pain and heartbreak, their spirits rearrange.

a chrysalis of sorrow, their hearts to endure,

a transformation miraculous, their spirits secure.

the healing that follows, a sanctuary of love,

the balm for their wounds, a gift from above.

with wings of transformation, their spirits take flight,

a testament to courage, their heart's delight.

- wings of transformation

a river that flows, through the passage of time,

the resilience of women, a strength to enshrine.

through the currents of sorrow, their spirits emerge,

a force to be reckoned, their hearts to surge.

the healing that follows, a torrent of grace,

the soothing of wounds, their hearts to embrace.

a river of resilience, forever to flow,

their spirits unyielding, their love to bestow.

- river of resilience

a garden that blooms, with love and with care,

the nurturing of women, their hearts to prepare.

through trials and tribulations, their spirits stand tall,

a testament to resilience, their love to enthrall.

the healing that follows, a balm to restore,

the wounds of the past, their hearts to adore.

a garden of nurturing, forever to grow,

their spirits embraced, their love to bestow.

- garden of nurturing

a beacon of light, in the darkness of night,

the hope of women, their spirits ignite.

through the storms of despair, their courage remains,

a lighthouse of hope, their hearts to sustain.

the healing that follows, a haven of peace,

the soothing of wounds, their hearts to release.

a lighthouse of hope, forever to shine,

their spirits united, their love to entwine.

- lighthouse of hope

a quilt lovingly sewn, with threads of devotion,

the compassion of women, their hearts in motion.

through the chill of heartache, their spirits warm,

a quilt of compassion, their love to transform.

the healing that follows, a blanket of care,

the mending of wounds, their hearts to repair.

a quilt of compassion, forever to bind,

their spirits enfolded, their love to remind.

- the quilt of compassion

a symphony resounding, with notes of love,

the sisterhood of women, their spirits above.

through the cacophony of heartache, their harmony
rings,

a symphony of sisterhood, their hearts to sing.

the healing that follows, a melody to mend,

the soothing of wounds, their hearts to tend.

a symphony of sisterhood, forever to play,

their spirits united, their love to convey.

- symphony of sisterhood

a bridge spanning chasm, of pain and despair,

the understanding of women, their hearts to repair.

through the gorges of heartbreak, their spirits ascend,

a bridge of understanding, their love to extend.

the healing that follows, a path to reconcile,

the soothing of wounds, their hearts to beguile.

a bridge of understanding, forever to stand,

their spirits connected, their love hand in hand.

- bridge of understanding

a tree rooted deeply, in the soil of life,

the wisdom of women, their spirits through strife.

through the seasons of sorrow, their branches grow strong, a tree of wisdom, their hearts to belong.

the healing that follows, a shelter of peace,

the mending of wounds, their hearts to release.

a tree of wisdom, forever to thrive,

their spirits enlightened, their love to survive.

in the pages of time, their stories unfold,

the tales of women, their strength to uphold.

through pain and heartbreak, their spirits renew,

a journey of healing, their hearts to pursue.

the words that we share, a balm to appease,

the wounds of the past, their hearts to release.

embrace the resilience, the love to entwine,

the spirits of women, forever to shine.

- tree of wisdom

About the book

"Being a Lady" is a powerful and moving collection of poetry written by Top G. Through his carefully crafted words, Top G provides a window into the hearts and minds of women, exploring the complexities of their lives and experiences. From the pain of heartbreak to the joy of self-discovery, Top G's writing delves deep into the emotional landscape of womanhood. His work is both raw and honest, resonating with readers who have felt unseen and unheard. "Being a Lady" is a tribute to the resilience and strength of women everywhere, and a testament to the power of poetry to move and inspire. Whether you are a fan of poetry or simply looking for a heartfelt and authentic read, "Being a Lady" is not to be missed.

About the author

Top G is a renowned poet hailing from Romania. With a deep understanding of women and the struggles they face, he has captured their pain and emotions in his writing. His debut book, "Being a Lady," is a testament to his ability to empathize and connect with his readers.

Top G's words are both powerful and compassionate, as he strives to give voice to those who have been silenced. His writing has touched the hearts of many, making him a highly respected figure in the literary world.

www.ingramcontent.com/pod-product-compliance
Lightning Source LLC
Chambersburg PA
CBHW070937120626
46546CB00004B/1450